Starships 101:

Basic Design Elements

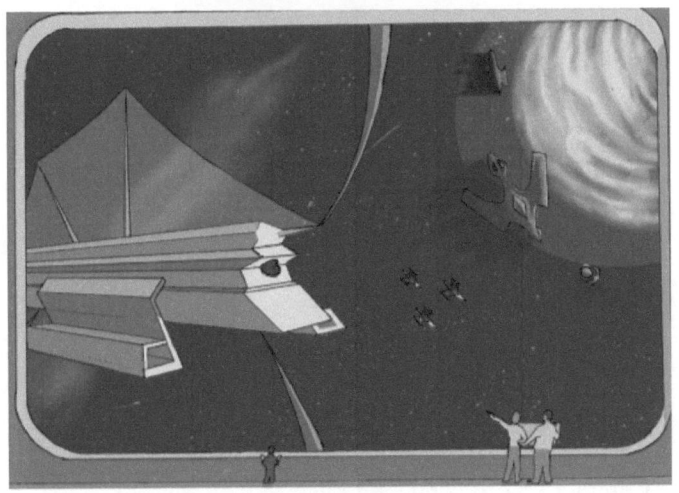

By Fred Files

Cover art by Marshall Lakes

Table of Contents

What is a Starship?

Spacecraft are real; Starships are not. Spacecraft are things of science that demonstrate man's desire and ability to push the limits of knowledge. Today spacecraft are current, achievable, and able to carry man into space around the Earth, and its moon while unmanned craft are exploring the solar system and beyond.

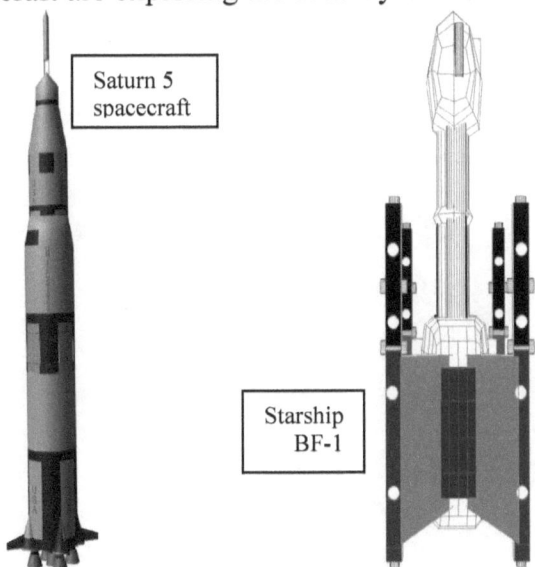

Saturn 5 spacecraft

Starship BF-1

Starships are imaginary things of fiction; they reach beyond today's achievable goals, they are ships designed to sail between the stars. They cross galaxies and travel between universes in the blink of an eye. Starships can be elegant or ugly, small or large; regardless of their form they carry the imagination to places beyond the limits of reality. Bold men and women crew these starships going out to explore space, defend Earth, and give birth to new legends. Or starships and their crews may be much more limited in capability, depending on the rules and history of the universe and story the Starship is in. In either case, the Starship is what a Spacecraft aspires to someday be.

Even a thing of fiction like a Starship can be improved if a little thought is put into its design and concept, and that is the purpose behind this book.

External Design

When designing a starship the first step is to establish the concept of the ship, what was the original purpose of the ship? Once that is established it can be used to determine the basic size the ship, and what capabilities the ship would need to fulfill that purpose.

For example the needs of a Freighter would focus on cargo capacity and engine power to move the cargo's mass. A medical ship would have extensive medical facilities, and a life support system capable of handling a much larger capacity than the regular crew. Survey ships have an extensive sensor suite. Other ships may be built in order to accommodate a combination of different rolls, although it would not be able to do any of them as well as a ship designed specifically for a given task… at least not for the same economic cost.

The next step is to ask if that is still the ships purpose, and how would the ship have been modified to fulfill its new roll. How would a freighter be altered into a combat vessel; a medical ship into a troop transport, a survey ship into an interceptor, or into an advance scout? Another consideration is what capabilities will the story require the ship to have?

Once the function has been determined the shape of the ship can be determined. Shape and form don't have that much relevance since aerodynamics doesn't matter in space; it can look like anything. If the ship is suppose to be able to operate within a planet's atmosphere, then that should be reflected in its design, with landing gear ports, wings or winglets, and a more aerodynamic design. If the ship is to be able to land in water or operate under water, then that too should be reflected in the design.

How the ship is constructed should also be considered, as that will greatly influence the look of the ship. If the culture building the ship is advanced in biological sciences, the ship could be grown organically. The advantages would be quicker control responses, and a built in level of self-repair, but it would be much harder to alter or upgrade the ship after it has been constructed. If a ship is not organic then it almost certainly has to be constructed in a construction dock either on a planet or in space out of metal or ceramic materials. The starship can look like anything, it can either have a purely functional design, or it can be stylized to resemble any motif imaginable.

Some ships are constructed modularly; their components built on earth or elsewhere and then assembled in space. This method of construction makes changing the capabilities of the ship as easy as switching out one module with another one. Unfortunately Modularly constructed ships are more fragile. Ships constructed in docks can also be built with some modular sections that can be switched out to change the ship's function.

Next is the overall design of the ship; linier construction is a method of designing a ship from front to back. The engines are typically on the side or in back, weapons are on the top or sides, while the bridge is in front or on top. These ships are generally very sturdy and powerful compared to modular ships, but the localized nature of each section or department makes for vulnerabilities.

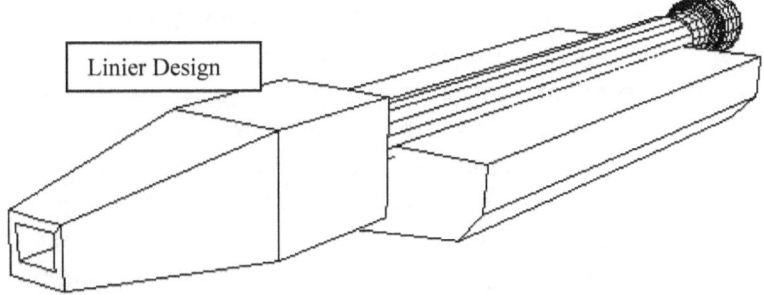

Linier Design

The opposite of Linier construction is decentralized construction. These would be your typical flying saucer, extremely agile and maneuverable because there is not a single engine giving thrust, but engines all about the exterior of the ship all capable of providing the same level of thrust. That means it does not have a central engine, but many; as well as many different control centers. The advantage being an endless level of redundancy among all systems, there is always another three engines to take over if one should be disabled. The draw back is that so much space and power must be dedicated to these redundant systems that less

room is available for specialized systems…
unless of course, the ship is massive.

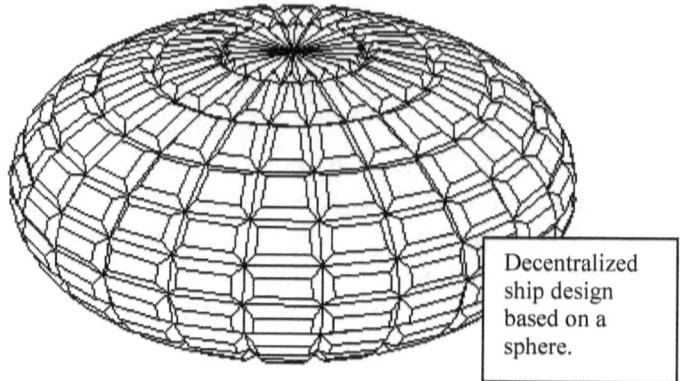

Decentralized
ship design
based on a
sphere.

The interior design of the ship should also be
considered while designing the outside, to
prevent continuity errors. Where is the Bridge
located? Where is Engineering? Is it close
enough to the Engines and the power supply?
Where are the Hanger bays? If the ship were
attacked, what areas would be easiest to damage?
Where would boarding parties most likely come
aboard? Are the weapon mounts positioned to
defend the ship from any angle?

If the ship is being designed for a game, or
simple story, then the interior layout really does
not need to be considered; but if the ship is going
to feature heavily or will be a center point for a
while then more of the ships interior and
construction should be considered. The
following pages will go into greater detail of
departments, rooms, and equipment that
starships should have, as well as potential
technologies that could be used in their
construction. While the precise location of each
of them is not necessarily important, one should

keep in mind their locations in relationship with each other.

Starship Organization

The most important thing on a starship is the Captain of the ship. He is the guiding force behind the ship, and must make decisions based on information that is relayed to him from the other departments. The captain does not see the fully detailed picture unless he wants to or needs to, and typically won't have time for that. The various departments take their specialized areas of information and filter it down so that the captain can have a condensed but accurate picture of everything that is going on in and around the ship.

The Departments include:

> Command
> Armory
> Brig
> Cargo Support
> Communications
> Computer
> Damage Control
> Engineering
> Fire Control
> Hanger bay
> Helm/Navigation
> Life Support
> Medical
> Personnel Support Systems
> Science
> Security

Command Department

All of the information to and from the Captain comes together on the ship's Main Bridge, or Command Deck. The possible layouts of the bridge are limitless, but the two most popular layouts are either circular with the Captain at the center surrounded by officers manning the various stations; or in a linier configuration similar to the command deck of a submarine. Each Bridge station is tied directly to one of the other departments.

Regardless of the Bridge configuration, there is the Captain's Chair. The captain's chair is not special because of its location, or added padding, but because it has easy access to duplicate controls or readouts from the other bridge stations. That enables the captain to keep a closer eye on what is going on, and to take over for an officer if they become incapacitated.

Most ships will have more than one Bridge. The First Bridge is the one that is most commonly used for daily use. In cases of extreme danger, or if something happens to the first Bridge, command is transferred to the Second or Combat Bridge. The Second Bridge is generally much smaller than the primary one, and located in a much more secure location, it is always staffed, ready to take over from the first Bridge at a moments notice, because if it is necessary for the

Second Bridge to take over, there may be no advance notice.

Larger ships will also have a Third Bridge, or a Flag Bridge, which is much larger than the First and Second Bridge; it also contains additional scanning and communications equipment. In the event of a Flag officer being on the ship, they can take command of the Flag Bridge and use its facilities to monitor and command fleet actions and guide the fleet without worrying about their specific ship, which is still being guided by the Captain on the First or Second Bridge. If something should happen to the Captain or the First and Second Bridge the Flag Bridge is still capable of controlling the ship. Note: Flag Officers can do whatever they want, if they want to take over as Captain while worrying about the rest of the fleet, they can, and the Captain won't have a say in the matter.

Armory

The Armory is where a majority of the weaponry used by the crew is stored. Not just simple pistols used for defending the ship from boarding parties, but any weapons that the ship's crew may possibly need to complete any missions are stored here. It is more than just a warehouse, as techs constantly maintain and repair the weapons to make sure they are all in perfect working order. Ammunition and missiles for any fighters the ship may carry would also be cared for by the Armory personnel, but stored in a separate place, near the hanger. Not all of the guns used by the

16

ship's crew will be stored in the armory, some will be stored in secured weapon lockers located in key parts of the ship so that the crew can get at them easily in case they need to defend themselves against boarding parties.

The location of the Armory should be carefully considered, as it must both be readily accessible by security to defend the ship and crewmembers that must equip themselves for missions, but the Armory must also be easy to defend against boarding parties or even mutineers.

Although the Armory is listed as it's own department, it is actually under the Security Department and does not usually report directly to the Bridge.

Brig

The Brig also falls under the Security department, and is not likely to be continuously staffed, unless the ship has a prisoner. The Brig is the ship's prison, each cell is small and sparse, small ships wont even bother to have one, and the average ship is not likely to have a large Brig. The cells could have either a solid door or a force field, although the force field is not recommended if there is the slightest chance of a power failure. The Brig needs to be designed to both contain the prisoners within it in the event of a riot and break out, and defended from any hoping to break the prisoners out. On the other hand, if the brig is destroyed in ship-to-ship combat, it may not be that big a loss.

The Brig design must also take into account the safety of visitors to the prisoners. Some Brigs also are equipped with facilities for interrogation, and not always the gentle kind.

Cargo Support

All Starships come quipped with cargo bays for storing ship provisions, and for transporting supplies from one place to another. It is a simple enough concept, except that there must be cargo handlers to move the cargo and secure it in place. The Ships provisions must be constantly inventoried and rationed out so that there is no chance of the ship running out of food in the middle of nowhere. Cargo must also be carefully monitored to make sure that stasis chambers don't break down, or that items that are temperature sensitive are maintained at their proper temperatures. In addition, it would be an embarrassing mistake if the ship offloaded the wrong cargo by mistake.

Communications

Space, especially in more populated regions is flooded with communication and navigation signals transmitted on thousands of different frequencies, in hundreds of different methods and in hundreds of different forms of encoding. The Communications department must monitor all of these frequencies and separate a call from a new culture on a new planet from a thousand year Earth television broadcast. The trash is either cataloged or discarded, while the rest is brought to the attention of either the Captain or the Science Department for analysis.

The Communications department also handles all personal calls to and from the crewmembers, although much of that level of communications can be automated.

Language translation is another aspect of the Communications department, having either linguists or translation programs for as languages as possible, as well as code breaking programs for decoding messages.

The physical location of the Communications department does not need any special placement, as long as it is away from any nosier systems like the engines.

Computer Department

Networking and miniaturization of computer components has removed the need for a central computer room to locate all of a ships computer system. In addition, if the central computer room was damaged it would cripple the ship completely. Instead the computer systems can be located anywhere with redundant memory located in different servers, some in rooms, and others in the walls of corridors.

Computer Rooms do still exist, not as the central computer core, but as a secure area for information. Top Secret information, like military star charts can only be accessed in the computer room, or possibly by the captain's own personal terminal. Computer rooms also contain all the information needed to reprogram the entire ships systems in case of virus infection, or if an EMP damages computer functions.

The Computer Room is EMP shielded, and as an additional precaution keeps all data backed up on media that can not be effected by outside energies; such as on CD ROMS or metallic punch-cards. It should be located in a heavily shielded location and the Security Department limits access to the room to Computer Department personnel and people authorized for the information they are requesting.

The actual Computer department personnel operate the computers in the Computer Room, as well as maintain the computer systems and programs in the entire ship.

The Computer Department answers to both the Science Department, and Damage Control.

Damage Control

Damage Control is one of the most dangerous departments there is on board a starship, since they frequently work in unstable areas and under unstable conditions. As the name implies, their job is to repair any damage done to the ship. Normally there is not excessive risk, aside from space walks the need to enter unsafe areas, combating fires, and dealing with and in radioactive items.

Combat situations are where a good Damage Control department really shines, as they are called on to carryout repairs even as the ship is under fire and taking damage. If the Radar or Engine Systems are damaged, the survival of the ship could easily depend on how quickly Damage Control got those systems operating again.

Occasionally Damage Control teams may be loaned out to assist with problems on other ships. Damage Control has to work with most of the other departments, calling on the Computer Department for specialized repairs and they assist and are assisted by members of the Engineering Department.

Engineering

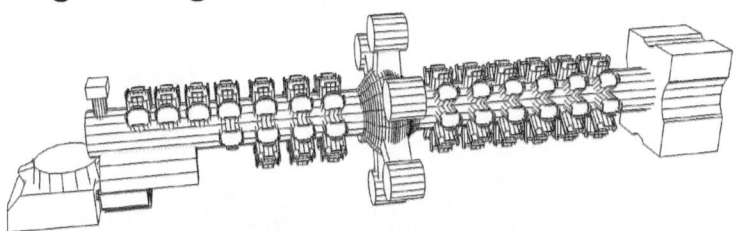

The engineering department monitors, maintains and operates the ship's power and propulsion systems. When making repairs to these systems, the Engineering Department is called on for their expertise to work with or as Damage Control, but mainly on just those systems.

The majority of the Engineering Department operates in the Engineering room, located in or near either the Engine Room or the Reactor. The Engineering room has all the equipment necessary to monitor and control both the Reactor and Engines; the engines and reactors themselves are too large, noisy and hazardous environments to be a practical location for the Engineering Department.

Engineering makes sure the ships power needs are met, and works with the Navigation Department to actually steer the ship. Types of power sources and engines will be covered in another section.

Fire Control

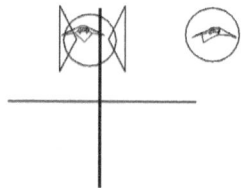

Fire Control essentially controls all of the starships offensive and targeting systems. The department makes use of the Sensor and Scanner data taken in by the Science department and identifies and locates ships and other objects around the ship. The location information is then used to target those objects with weapons, tractor beams, or other systems.

Fire Control also maintains the ships weapons systems, except for those maintained by the Armory; and Damage Control handles larger repairs. The weapons systems available can include Missiles, Torpedoes, projected energy, or solid projectile weapons. They also control some defensive weapons such as interceptors, and pin-point barrier shields.

Hanger Bay

On ships large enough to have one, the Hanger Bay is located near outer hull of the ship, with a door or airlock leading out to space. It typically consists of at least two rooms, the launch bay where smaller ships launch or land, and a second hanger area where the ships are safely stored until needed. Some ships also contain launch tubes for rapid deployment of fighters. The Hanger contains any fighters, Shuttles, or other transports that the ship is likely to need to complete its missions.

These smaller ships need pilots as well as people to maintain, refuel and store these ships, as well as to assist them in landing and launching the ships. Launch operations at least need someone to inform the pilot that the area outside the ship is clear of obstacles, usually from the bridge using tracking information provided by the Fire Control Department. Depending on technologies, someone may also need to cycle the air lock so the smaller craft can get out. More advanced ships have air shields that keep the atmosphere within the hanger bay, but allow ships to pass through into the void of space.

Landing operations at least require an observer to make sure the landing craft is coming in at the proper direction and speed, or for more complicated landing systems, someone needs to operate the Tractor Beam or tow cables to bring the smaller ship into the starships hanger.

Helm/Navigation

Helm and Navigation control the starships movements. Navigation specializes in stellar-cartography and may have an entire area dedicated to mapping stars, pulsars, black holes and other spatial landmarks. The main job of Navigation is to use these landmarks to pinpoint the starships current position, and plot a course to the ships intended destination. The information used by navigation comes from the ships Science Department.

The Helm section controls the ships movements by giving instructions to Engineering or by direct control of the engines and directional thrusters. They make sure the ship stays on the course set by Navigation, and avoid hitting any obstacles in the ships path. Helm focuses on closer objects that may damage the ship, information provided by Fire Control.

Life Support

Each Department, and piece of equipment on a starship needs someone to run it, depending on the size of the ship and the level of technology available, that could come to a large number, but that number is also limited by the ships ability to sustain that number of people.

Life Support provides the basic necessities for the crew, specifically air, water, and gravity. Life Support maintains whatever systems generate atmosphere if it is stored air run through filters to keep it fresh, or if air is generated through gardens on the ship. Water also could either be stored whole or in component elements to be reformed when it is needed, or acquired through some other method. Gravity, if present at all could be generated with rotating sections, as a byproduct of a Gravity Drive propulsion system, or through some other method.

Generally the maximum crew capacity of a starship is determined less by space and more by the limits of Life Support to maintain them.

Food is another major consideration of Life Support, and is sometimes tied to oxygen production if it uses gardens. The crew must eat, and food must be stored or grown and prepared for them.

Medical

An unavoidable fact is that people get sick and injured, and that must be accommodated for. Colds, plagues, cuts, severe burns, anything is possible when encountering the unknown, or in a combat situation. A small starship may have nothing more than a first-aid kit, while larger ships may be equipped with the equivalent of a full hospital.

Another function of the Medical Department is the decontamination of any crewmembers that leave the ship for unknown or suspected environments. Decontamination is not only against radiation, but to check against any parasites, viruses, or other bacteria that could possibly spread to other crewmembers.

Personnel Support Systems

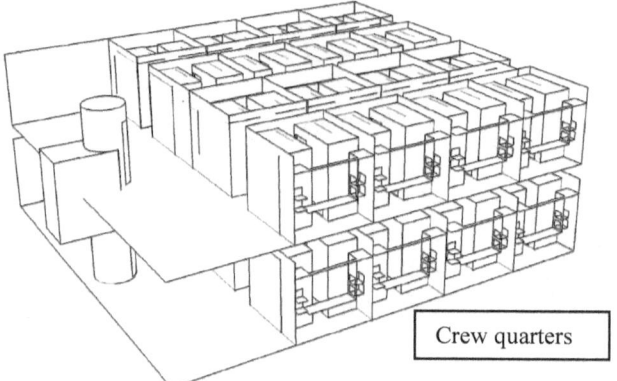

Crew quarters

Personnel Support is very closely tied to certain aspects of the Life Support department. While Life Support handles air, water, gravity and the things needed to keep the Crew alive; Personnel

Support provides the facilities that make life aboard ship livable, and the crew to keep the facilities running. Cooks to prepare the food provided by Life Support; quarters and or bedding for the crew to sleep; laundry service for uniforms; recreation facilities such as Gymnasiums and Holography Rooms; Showers; or virtually anything else needed to live on the Starship.

Science

The Science department makes the most use of the ships sensors and scanners, and has other labs to do whatever chemical analysis maybe required. The most common activity is to take data constantly being received by the sensors and assemble that information into an accurate picture of what lies outside the ship, or within the ship if circumstances call for it, and to relay that information to the captain and crew in a way they will understand.

The end result is that if the ship should come across any unusual stellar phenomena or creature then the Science Department is relied on interpret the information to explain what, how and why... and to provide solutions to prevent, stop, counteract, help, or duplicate such phenomena or creature.

Security

A utopian universe would have no need for a Security Department. The security department keeps the ship secure; to do so it provides protection from any possible hostile threats such as internal threats like mutiny or spies, or external threats like boarding parties. The main method the Security department uses is through manpower; providing guards to keep watch over away missions, and to guard secure areas of the ship, and by providing troops to combat invaders, or to execute more aggressive actions. Security personnel are more likely to be equipped with a firearm than any other members of the crew.

In addition to personnel, the Security Department also has passive deterrents at their disposal, in the ability to halt an intruder's progress by deploying shields or blast doors, or by activating automated weapon systems. Under extreme circumstances, the Security department may work with Life Support to evacuate atmosphere from sections of the ship to provide an added level of protection by killing anyone in an unprotected area not wearing a spacesuit.

Security has access to just about any weapons in the ships Armory, but must select what weapons they use with care. It would be unfortunate if a security officer accidentally caused explosive decompression in a chamber by putting a hole in the wall, so they are unlikely to use a weapon with armor piercing or any real metal penetrating power while onboard the ship, while off the ship they may need to utilize something with much greater stopping ability.

A note about side arms, there are three places one usually wears a side arm… in a shoulder holster, on the hip under their dominant hand, or on the hip opposite the dominant hand. Worn on the shoulder, the weapon will not get in the way of whatever chair the crewman is sitting in, and the chair will not get in the way of pulling the side arm. Under the dominant hand, cowboy style accommodates the fast draw if the crewman is likely to be standing, while wearing it on the opposite hip, requiring a cross draw requires additional motion while standing, but can be pulled more easily while in a seated position… depending on the design of the chair and holster.

Starship Equipment

The previous section listed within the
departments some of the equipment and facilities
that department requires in order to function.
This section will go on to mention other
equipment that most starships will have standard.

Defensive Equipment

These systems allow the ship to protect itself from enemies and the elements.

Hull

The hull is the final, and weakest level of protection on a ship. It is strong enough to keep the atmosphere of a ship inside, and space outside, and that's about the extent of the expectations of the hull. If the ship is capable of entering an atmosphere or aquatic operation, then it is also expected to keep the ship from being crushed by the added pressure of an outside atmosphere or water.

Armor

Armor is the next level of protection. Its goal is to protect the hull from damage by enemy fire, micrometeorites or other physical or energy impacts. Some armor is reflective, or has a reflective layer intended to deflect or disperse laser impacts away from the ship.

Deflection fields

"Deflectors" are weak shields that don't try to forcibly stop damage from an attack, but are angled in an attempt to redirect the impact and damage away from the ship. These shields are projected only a millimeter beyond the armor, right on the skin of the ship.

Shields

Shields are an energy bubble projected around the ship to protect it from energy and physical damage usually by absorbing it. The more power pumped into a shield system the more damage it can sustain, of course there are always attempts to circumvent an opponents shields by adjusting weapon frequencies or type so that they will be able to pass through the shield without effect.

Some shield systems are unable to protect the entire ship, in this case there are either overlapping shield systems to protect the entire ship, or movable shield "barriers" that can be moved to protect specific areas of the ship.

Navigational Deflection Fields

While not really a combat system, this system can be very important. It is essentially the starship equivalent of the train's cow scoop. Micrometeorites and other small particles could damage the ship if it hits them at high speeds, the Navigational Deflectors project a cone to push these items out of the way of the ship as it passes, but it is too weak to be effective against anything larger than a small rock.

Ram Scoops

A ram scoop is also not really a defensive system, but it is essentially the opposite of a Navigational Deflector. Some ships create their own fuel and water supply by scooping up space dust, nebulas, and the outer most levels of a planet's atmosphere. A Ram Scoop funnels that material into the ship to be processed and made into water or whatever else is needed.

Interceptors

Interceptors are the low-tech version of shields. It is a rapid firing cannon that fires a layer of flack to intercept and set off or deflect incoming fire. Targeting systems on interceptors must be first rate to target incoming laser or cannon fire to hit the oncoming stream before it strikes the ship.

Blast Doors

In the event that there is a hull breach, special heavy doors are located at the entry point of each room, and periodically along the corridors of the ship. These doors are heavily armored and radiation shielded, designed to seal off damaged sections of the ship so that the loss of atmosphere does not damage the rest of the ship. Sometimes Force Fields can be deployed to fill the same purpose.

Patching Systems

In addition to blast doors, additional patching systems can be deployed, these can be anything such as inflated balls that fly to the hole in the hull to block it, or a shield projected over the breach to contain the air and maintain structural integrity. This is only a short-term solution until

Damage Control can arrive to effect proper repair.

ECM/ECCM

Electronic Countermeasures and Electronic Counter Countermeasures are a form of electronic defense. The goal is to project electronic and scanner interference that will prevent the enemy's weapon systems from targeting the ship… at the same time they are using their ECM to do the same, while ECCM is being deployed to counteract the enemy's ECM.

Offensive Systems

As they say, the best defense is a good offence.

Offensive systems are the weapons of the starship, and respond to fire control commands. There are generally three different tiers of weapons on a starship.

The **Primary weapon** is a starship's most powerful weapon; a single weapon of awesome strength that requires the ship's entire power reserve (and then some) to operate. The result of this power requirement means that the ship is a powerless target while the weapon is being used and either before or after it is used. It either takes time to charge the capacitors to be able to use the weapon, or depending on its design, it would take a while after the weapon is used to restore power to the rest of the ship and reboot computer systems. This type of weapon system is not installed on most ships, only on the most powerful of starships.

Main Weapons are standard ship-to-ship guns. Normally too large and bulky to be used on quick moving small targets, but they are very powerful in their own right.

Secondary Weapons include a variety of types of smaller guns mounted on a starship to support the main weapon and protect the ship. The secondary weapons are weaker yet quicker weapons used to defend against fighters and incoming missiles and energy beams. They include anti-aircraft guns and interceptors.

Weapon Systems can include:

Ram

Going back to the earliest days of naval ship combat, sometimes the best way to destroy an enemy is to ram into it. So that this maneuver can be something other than a suicidal maneuver, some ships are equipped with a ramming attachment. It could be a simple pointed stick jutting out in front of the ship, or something more decorative such as a ram's head or maybe it is designed to resemble a knife blade. More often than not, these rams are designed to break off in the other ship, to allow the attacker to get away if the ram should become stuck.

Missiles/Torpedoes

Generally a lower tech form of weapon, kept around by the endless variety of nastiness that can be installed in their warheads. This weapon is launched and consists of an engine that propels it to target, and is possibly capable of maneuvering it around obstacles. In front of this engine is the Warhead, which could contain any of an unlimited number of kinds of weapons. The Warhead could be a simple explosive, radioactive or not; it could contain a laser that goes off slicing indiscriminately once it is close enough to the target; it could contain an

ECM/ECCM suite to play havoc with the enemy's electrical systems.

Projectile Weapons

These are also on the lower tech level of weaponry; they are simply guns, cannons, or gauss guns that fire a solid shell of metal or explosive to strike the enemy's ship. These are basic line of sight weapons.

Energy Weapons

Energy weapons include Lasers, Phased Energy Cannons, Wave Guns, Shock Cannons, Plasma projectors or whatever other form of energy can be harnessed and unleashed for destructive effect. The variety of energy weapons and ways to modify them is greater than projectile weapons, but they too are line of site weapons, and cannot easily be made to turn corners to strike their targets.

Power Systems

These systems power ships systems so to enable the starship to function.

Power systems are needed for the obvious reason; they provide energy needed to operate anything and everything. Any device that does anything requires a power source

Battery Power

Batteries store power for future use. They cannot recharge themselves, but must be recharged by one of the other power supplies.

They are intended as a secondary power supply only that can sustain a ship's emergency functions (lights, life support, and maneuvering thrusters) at times when the ship's main power supply is off-line or when all power is being directed to perform a special task such as reinforcing shields or boosting the power of a weapon. The batteries, when not in use, receive a steady charge from the main power source. While powering all ship functions they tend to last only a few hours, if only sued to power limited functions they can last several years.

Chemical Reactors

Chemical reactors generate power from reactors that occur between two normally stable chemicals that react with each other to produce energy. These reactors require a mixing chamber to generate the actual reaction, and two separate fuel tanks for each of the chemicals used by the reactor. The two things that users of a chemical reactor need to keep in mind are the need to refuel both kinds of chemicals when they get low, and they need to be sure not to confuse which chemical goes into which tank.

Contained Nature Power Sources

Zero gravity chambers and inertial dampers make it possible to contain and harness seemingly large and impossible natural phenomena that can then be tapped for power. The natural power source could be anything from an entire planet to a star or a black hole. The lifespan and power output of such devices is nearly limitless. Due to the nature of the power sources being contained, if containment is lost the vessel which had been containing it will suddenly find itself being contained and destroyed by the power source.

Fission or Fusion Reactors

Fission reactors operate by splitting atoms and harnessing the energy released by the reaction. The fission reactors also have a tendency to generate large amounts of heat, which must be regulated. Fusion reactors fuse atoms together to create energy but most do not need the same kind of cooling needs as fission reactors. Both types use radioactive materials, either for cooling, fuel or waste by-product; exposure to the radioactive waste can result in death, but not always immediate. Although it requires more fuel for its reactions than fission, fusion is often preferred because it creates less waste.

Ships frequently use a combination of both fission and fusion reactors…. They are safe to shut down and will usually not explode in combat situations. Waste from fission reactors can easily be dropped into stars or black holes, and additional fuel for fusion reactors can be gathered out of the vastness of space itself, especially in nebula and near planets.

Matter/Anti-matter Reactors

Matter/anti-matter reactors work by mixing matter with anti-matter in a controlled reaction. The matter and anti-matter annihilate each other as soon as they are brought into contact with each other, resulting in a tremendous release of energy. A bi polar crystal is most commonly used control the rate that the matter and anti-matter enter the reaction chamber to ensure that the reaction does not get out of control. If the crystal develops a flaw, however, the results could be catastrophic.

The problem with this form of reactor is in the containment of the anti-matter. It must be contained in a field so that it does not come into contact with anything except itself. Force fields or magnetic fields are common containment methods for anti-matter; but if containment is lost or if the reactor looses control of the reaction rate the resulting explosion will likely destroy the entire ship.

Organic Power Sources

Life itself creates power. Organic substances can be genetically grown with the thought of energy production as its primary purpose. Although it seems natural for this type of power source to be used in an organically grown ship; organic power supplies can be utilized to power mechanically based ships.

Organic power sources do need food to sustain itself; this could be air, light, waste products, or anything.

Solar Power

Solar power is energy taken from the sun, usually by solar panels, although chemical coverings may also be used. The Key to solar power is that the more power you need, the larger the panels/treated surfaces must be. The performance of this power source is dependant on the presence of a sun or star to provide that power. Starships who travel great distances are unable to use solar power as a primary energy supply, but may use it to recharge the ship's batteries.

Propulsion Systems

These systems make the ship go.

Directional Thrusters

These are located at key points all across the ship, they assist with high speed maneuvering, but the time they are most useful is to position the ship or change its heading while the ship is moving at slow speeds or is stopped. These can be small jet thrusters or air or steam vents that open to give the ship a needed nudge.

Sub-light Engines

These are the engines used most often, especially in combat situations. They move the ship by providing forward thrust, but they are limited by the laws of physics. Some examples include:

Reaction Drives: these are basically large thrusters providing force in one direction to push the ship in the other.

Sails: Large sails, similar to sea-going sailing ships in form and function, are mounted on a ship to catch "solar winds." A system of laser beams projected from point to point can provide an interstate highway system for ships with sails to use.

FTL

Faster Than Light [FTL] drives do not necessarily obey the laws of physics; they are what allow the starship to travel between stars and galaxies fast enough for the crew to survive the trip.

The natures of FTL drives vary greatly depending on the technology being used:

"Light Speed"

"Light Speed" is going faster than the speed of light, but this causes a time shift where the people doing the traveling age slower than those not traveling at or beyond the speed of light. This allows people who doe a lot of traveling to remain young while their great grand children grow old and die.

Hyperspace

Hyperspace is a separate dimension that ships can travel within that allows them to reach destinations quicker than traveling through real space. Hyperspace can be entered by opening a hole into it, either with the ships own engines or by entering a form of gate that opens the hole for the ship. Gravity currents may exist within hyperspace and similar dimensions; ships that can navigate these currents can travel even faster.

Hyperspeed

Hyperspeed relies on speed to create something similar to a separate dimension for quicker travel, but objects that exist in the regular world, such as planets or stars are just as real, so courses must be plotted to avoid them. Most ships that use this form of FTL have gravity detectors that automatically disengage the engines when they detect the gravity field of such an obstruction.

Skip Warp

Skip Warping is a process of making several rapid and continuous mini-space warps. The end result is a ship that is going extremely fast, and to an outside observer, the ship will seem to have a strobe effect.

Space Fold

Space Folds allow starships to travel by literally creating a fold in space. Matter at the starting point of the fold is picked up and transferred to the second point of the fold.

Warp Bubble

Warp bubbles are formed by creating a bubble of subspace or some other dimension around a ship, which allows it to move much more quickly through regular space. The bubble allows the ship to warp several of the laws of physics, generating faster than light travel.

Warp Skip

A Warp Skip is slightly more complicated than most warps, the distance warped is determined by the amount of power and inertia the warping ship has when it begins the warp. The faster the ship is going when it warps, the further it will go.

Worm Hole

Worm Holes are tunnels that link one point in space to another. There is usually no visual way to locate a worm hole unless it is in use; they are often discovered by accident. Useful worm holes are stable, meaning a clear path that doesn't change. Unstable worm holes shift positions at one end or the other randomly; or will shred anything that enters them. Some theorize that black holes can act as Worm Holes or that worm holes can be artificially created.

Inertial Dampeners

This system is not really a method of propulsion but is included here as it is related. When the ship accelerates quickly, or changes direction suddenly then like a car or train, the crew would be thrown about, knocked off their feet, or turned into an icky puddle on the wall. Inertial Dampeners act to lessen the laws of inertia so that the crew does not experience the effect of the ships sudden movements or acceleration. In the event of attack or something the ships computers cant predict, then the crew would experience some jostling but not the full effect that they would without them. If something were to happen to take the Inertial Dampeners offline however, the results could be disastrous, and messy.

Miscellaneous Systems

A ship needs to do more than just defend, shoot and move around.

Airlocks

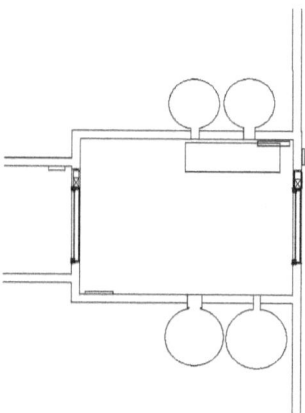

Airlocks are airtight chambers that are designed to allow one to enter/exit the ship without loss of atmosphere. A crewmember enters the chamber, puts on a space suit, the air cycles out, and then the other end of the chamber opens allowing the crewmember to exit into space. The process is reversed to return to the ship. Airlocks may also be located in the medical bay, to allow doctors to safely enter quarantine wards without risk of spreading disease to the rest of the ship. Airlocks can also be used for execution, by placing the victim in the airlock and cycling it without giving them protective wear. Airlocks may also be equipped with a bypass command that will allow them to open without going through the full cycling process... but airlocks are set so that both ends can never be open at the same time.

Beacons

Beacons are small satellites or marker buoys that a ship can leave behind them to accomplish different tasks. They can be set to mark locations; warn people away from a quarantined world; distress signal complete with a copy of the ships logs; some are designed to mimic the ships energy signatures to act as a decoy.

Decontamination

Decontamination chambers are under the responsibility of the Medical department. There should be one located in the Medical bay, as well as in the hanger or wherever crewmembers return to the ship after visiting other places. Any crewmembers who may have been exposed to unknown or alien viruses or bacteria are expected to go through a Decontamination chamber which is designed to scan for and remove any foreign materials, bacteria, viruses or radiation from the crewman. Failure to do so could result in a shipboard plague. If there is an infection that the Decontamination chamber cannot detect, then there is the potential for real trouble. It is important to note that a Decontamination chamber cannot cure someone who is already sick, only remove from him or her what may make him or her sick before hand.

Docking Port

Docking Ports are one half of a larger airlock, the other half being a docking port on another ship. When the ships dock together connecting the Docking Ports they work together to cycle air into the resulting boarding tube to allow people to move from one ship to the other. Docking ports are also used to connect to stations.

Escape Pods

Escape pods are located throughout the outer hull of the ship, they are the lifeboats of space, a small ship able to hold a small number of crewmembers and keep them alive for a short amount of time. If the order to abandon ship is given, the crews get into the nearest escape pods, which eject from the ship when they are full. The escape pods get a safe distance away from the ship, and provided it is safe to do so, activate a distress signal and wait for help. If a habitable planet is nearby they are capable of landing, but not necessarily of taking off again. Escape pods will be mentioned again in the ship types section.

Gravity

Artificial Gravity on board a ship makes living much easier... as well as helping the general health of a crew of people not designed to live in a zero gravity environment. Some ships achieve artificial gravity by having rotating sections to generate gravity, while the rest of the ship goes without. More advanced ships use various other methods to achieve artificial gravity.

Intraship Transportation

On ships, especially large ships, the crew may need help getting from one area to the next quickly, even if the crew is quartered near their duty stations, so equipment is installed to make travel within the ship quicker. This could include trams that shuttle crewmembers or pilots from one area to another, quick-tubes to slide from one level to the next, and lifts to provide quick transportation from one section of the ship to another.

Observation Deck

Purely optional, the observation deck is dedicated to giving the ships passengers and crew the most stunning view of space outside the ship as possible. It in its most basic form, this is a room with massive windows. This is a must for civilian passenger liners, whose passengers want to see the romantic beauty of space while they travel. Observation Decks can also double as lounges or mess halls.

Probes

Probes are specialized missiles that instead of containing explosives contain a sensor suite to extend the ships own sensor range, and send the data back to the ship. To this end, a probe also has a longer range that a typical missile as well.

Space Suit Lockers

Space suits lockers should be located near each airlock to for easy access. However due to the hazardous nature of space and unpredictability of combat situations portions of the ship may be exposed to vacuum, so space suits should also be available at other locations through out the ship.

Tractor Beam/Grapple

Occasionally the ship may need to tow something, either another ship, a cargo container, or maybe an asteroid. Tractor Beams are energy beams that attract their targets to the ship, careful use of these beams and thrust allow the ship to tow items or pull them towards the ship. If the technology needed to generate such a beam is not available, then grappling hooks or harpoons may be used instead.

Starship Disasters

There are some situations that can all too easily spell doom for a starship, and those situations must be avoided at all costs.

Dead Zones

Dead Zones are sections of space that have been dimensionally torn, or for whatever reason different in that the mechanics that make FTL drives work will not function in that area of space. The only way through is by slow sub light engines. Some of these zones are accompanied by either high gravity to render sub light engines worthless or some other property that saps energy from the ship. In many cases these zones have become Starship Graveyards, filled with alien ships who have fallen prey, unable to leave, their crews dead through old age, suicide or starvation.

Explosive Decompression

Air on a starship is constantly trying to expand, and is only held in place by the hull of the ship. If the material making the hull should become weakened, or develop a small hole, all of the air in the compartment will attempt to rush out into space with explosive result, widening the hole even more. This is called Explosive

Decompression, when the air explodes out, taking parts of the ship with it. When this happens it can cause a chain reaction, as the air in the adjoining compartments take advantage of the sudden drop in pressure along one wall to find previously hidden weak points in the walls or hull, and explode out themselves. The resulting chain reaction of damage can be catastrophic.

Some forms of combat between ships rely heavily on Explosive Decompression, all the ship weapons attempt to do is weaken the hull or make tiny holes and allow Explosive Decompression to do the rest of the work, destroying the starship.

Fire

In a contained environment such as a starship fire has no place to go except to follow the air, burning everything even metal, therefore there is no place for the crew to escape to. Fire fighters fight the fires as best they can by trying to flood it out, having to smother the entire thing, or at least make a path for them to get through and to keep the fire away from dangerous or explosive equipment. The quickest way to put out a fire is to evacuate the oxygen from the sections exposing it to vacuum, however all crew must be evacuated out of the area first. Fire also weakens the structural integrity of the walls in the effected area so exposing the area to vacuum could result in explosive decompression.

Plague

Because a starship is an enclosed environment, disease can travel very quickly from person to person, in the recycled air supply, and in the re-filtered water. Filters and decontamination technologies are in place, but in the event that there is something that slips past them to affect the rest of the ship it can easily be very deadly. If it is something that is different enough to get past the ships sensors and filters then there is a good chance it wont be detected by the crews immune systems, possibly killing them easily.

Voids

Voids are a navigational hazard, not always detectable before entering one. They are caused by magnetic clouds or other phenomena, but the end result is a magnetic abyss that distorts space, depriving the starship of any navigational landmarks, and frequently disabling any long distance communication as well. Often visual fixes are also impossible as even visual light can be distorted into pitch-blackness.

Starship Classes

The following is a listing of starship types, sorted by size. Small Craft cover one-man ships up to ships with a small passenger load. Midsize craft include what could be considered large private ships to small capitol ships. Capitol ships cover everything else from destroyers up through planet destroyers.

Small Craft

Escape Pods

This ship class ranges widely in size, at its smallest, it is smaller than a fighter, able to eject a fighter pilot to safety; at its largest they can be the size of a large shuttle, to assist in the evacuation of large capital ships.

Escape Pods contain an automatic distress beacon, and the most basic of propulsion systems, as well as life support and food supplies. Their purpose is to carry surviving crew and pilots away from immediate danger.

Fighter

Fighters are small and maneuverable combat ships containing the minimum equipment necessary to do their job. They are essentially weapon platforms with engines, and pilots. Most fighters are short range craft working in groups along side carriers, but fighters can be built with their own FTL drives to operate at greater distances.

Bombers

Bombers serve the same basic function as fighters; only their weapon systems are primarily for ground targets. They are built slightly larger for a heavier weapons payload of missiles and bombs.

Courier

This class specializes in relaying information, and information being small when stored on computer disks does not require much space, therefore these ships are built small and able to travel vast distances quickly, although they have weak defenses. If the technology level is high enough for FTL communication, then courier ships will be rare, as they would not be needed to relay communications except when secrecy is needed.

Shuttle

The main purpose of the shuttle is to transport people and cargo from a larger starship to another or to a planet. They can be equipped for long distance journeys as well, especially for situations when the main Starship is needed elsewhere.

Light Attack Craft (LAC)

LACs are essentially fighters that have been equipped with weaponry designed for capital ships. While they are larger and more powerful than fighters, and pack a massive punch for their size; they still have very little protection and are easily destroyed. Their weaponry is also limited by an energy system that is too weak to properly support the mounted weaponry. Each weapon mounted on a LAC will not be able to fire many times before needing to be recharged by a larger ship.

Midsize Craft

Gunship

The Gunship is the starship equivalent of a tank. The ship is built around a single primary weapon system with very little else in the way of armor or additional systems.

Freighter

Of all the ships designed to carry cargo, the freighter is the smallest (except for a cargo shuttle). It is intended for quick cargo runs when speed is more important than quantity.
Freighters are also used to ferry cargo off of bulk transports and down to planets/other ships/etc. The freighter is often the ship of choice for smugglers.

Survey Ship

This class of ship has a minimal size crew, with a bulk of the ship being dedicated to sensor equipment and cargo space for any samples that may be collected during a mission.

"Submarine"

Subs are stealth craft that can hide their appearance, either by hiding behind some form of stealth or cloaking technology, or by diving into another dimension or subspace. They are designed as either scout craft penetrating deep into enemy territory, or as attack craft mounting surprise attacks.

Sleeper Ship

Cultures that have not yet developed faster than light technologies may make use of long-range sleeper ships. The ship itself is largely automated with the passengers and crew spending the trip in suspended animation. Suspended animation is done so that the crew can survive a long trip of a hundred years or longer; or because the ship does not have the power or life support to support the crew for the entire journey.

Yacht

Yachts are personal transports, some are modified freighters, but others are designed specifically for the purpose of personal transportation.

Capitol Ships

Asteroid Ships

Asteroid ships are built from a midsize asteroid that is hollowed out to provide crew, control spaces, and engines are attached to the outside to provide movement. This ship type lends itself to secrecy, although it may require vast amounts of desperation.

Frigate/Destroyers

Frigates, or Destroyers are smaller combat vessels, designed to work in groups to provide protective escorts to other ships. They can also work alone on patrols, but they are not likely to survive an unfortunate encounter with anything larger than another destroyer. The ship class can be used for non-combat functions; to conduct surveys or other tasks that would not require a large ship.

Cruiser

This is the main workhorse class of ship, the size that can be configured to complete about any task necessary. They can be equipped with enough weapons to be a significant threat, or made into carriers, loaded with scientific gear for research missions, or they can be equipped with a variety of systems to make the ship able to do a little of anything, although nothing as well as a ship dedicated to that function.

Medical Ship

Medical ships specialize in mass evacuation and treatment of peoples in cases of disease plagues or disasters. They also include advanced biological and chemical research labs to perform on site testing and treatment. Many Medical ships are specially built, but some are modified frigates or cruisers.

Liners

Liners are luxury transports. They are used for vacation tours, casinos, and any other method of relaxing. They are the primary method of travel for civilians who need to get from one planet to another.

Battleships

Battleships are the ultimate warships, designed to take and dispense punishment. Many a fleet of destroyers and gunships has been obliterated when their fleet commanders miscalculated the amount of damage they could take within the time it would take them to destroy a battleship.

Carrier

Carriers are also warships, but carry a minimum of offensive or defensive weaponry, relying instead of a screen of fighter craft. The main purpose of a carrier is to transport, deploy and support fighters and other small starships.

Agricultural Ship

Most ships large enough to be considered a capitol ship contains at least a small hydroponics area to grow natural food and generate oxygen. Agricultural ships can perform that function for an entire fleet, or world. They are space-based greenhouses containing forests, fields and occasionally wildlife.

Exploration

Exploration ships are intended to explore and chart deep space. They are equipped to establish and monitor first contact situations and operate for extended periods of time without supply or support.

Colony

Colony ships are built for the sole purpose of planting a (semi-) self-supporting colony on another world. They carry a minimal crew as well as all the colonists and whatever supplies will be needed to start a new colony on a distant world. Some Colony ships are designed to be deconstructed into additional building supplies for the colony. The colony ship is also the colonists' one chance to return home if some disaster should befall the colony. Some colony ships also qualify as sleeper ships, and most generational ships are also used to place colonies.

Bulk Cargo Transport

Transports are cargo haulers, while the ships themselves may be huge, but when it comes to crew size and facilities they are actually quite small, the bulk of the ship is dedicated to cargo space, with large engines able to handle the increased mass of a heavy cargo load.

Q-Ship

Q-Ships are cargo transports or are designed to resemble transports, but they have been equipped with massive amounts of weaponry in place of cargo. They were originally developed as a trap for pirates who hunt slow moving and lightly armored cargo ships expecting an easy target only to be destroyed by a surprise attack from the Q-ship.

Dreadnaught

These are primarily combat ships, large and massive, with more overall power than even a battleship. Dreadnaughts are usually only built or operated during times of war.

Space Station

Not really a starship, a space station is a more or less stationary space construction that acts as a fort, trading post, or a refueling and repair yard for visiting starships. Space stations normally orbit planets, but can be placed anywhere… but it takes a lot of time or effort to move one once it has been placed. The largest stations can even act as a ship construction yard.

Generational Ship

Generational ships are a low-tech answer to long distance space flights. They are built extra large, in some cases large enough to simulate a planetary surface inside. The crew and colonists live on the ship, have children and then train their children to take over their jobs once they have gotten too old to carry on and die. This process repeats itself several times over as many generations as it takes for the ship to reach its destination.

Space Colonies

Not really a starship because they are largely stationary; Space colonies are normally started before it is technologically possible to reach other planets. They are essentially larger space stations, with many more luxury items such as "outdoor" housing and simulated weather patterns and mirror controlled "night" and "day." They do have a relatively small crew for their size, but their population is much larger than a typical space station. Colonies are crewed almost entirely by civilians.

Battle stations

Battle stations are closer to being starships than space stations because they are designed to be moved. They are the ultimate war machines; massive mobile space stations that have been ultra fortified and equipped with enough weaponry to take on just about anything. Once moved into position and accompanied by a fleet of support ships, they are nearly invincible.

Planet Destroyers

Also known as Doomsday Machines; these ships are intended to be the ultimate threat to ensure peace. If they are used then they can only escalate whatever conflict they are engaged in until there is nothing left of either side. As the name implies; a Planet Destroyer is a single weapon capable of destroying an entire planet with a single attack; some are capable of destroying entire planetary systems at a time by causing the system's sun to go nova. Planet Destroyers often must rely on stealth and smaller ships for defense as their entire make up is dedicated to destroying the single large target. These ships are big; often as large as a planet themselves.

Sample Missions

Patrol

Patrol missions are security work, the ship travels over a set area of space; it could be a trade route or a boarder between empires. The ship's goal is to find and remove any other ships that are not suppose to be there, this includes tracking down pirates laying in wait for cargo transports; hunting smugglers; and tracking down enemy ships that sneak across the boarders to spy or who plan to destroy a lone patrol ship.

Survey

Survey missions are the basic exploration missions; the starship travels deep into under explored areas of space and then uses its sensors to map out new stars, planets, and other stellar bodies. If necessary the ship also places navigation markers and communication relay satellites, and catalog potential sources of natural resources for future exploitation. The ship maps and catalogs unexplored planets, and must be prepared for first contact situations if it should encounter new space baring races. Some survey missions could be extra detailed such as assigning a ship to study a particular planet over a period of time collecting data on its culture, life forms, seasons, and every other aspect of the world.

Transport

Transportation missions can call for a wide variety of ship types depending on what is being transported. Information or communications would need a small fast ship capable of traveling vast distances quickly. Military style personnel transport would just need life support and defenses; while civilian personnel transports would either be something like an intergalactic bus, or a luxury liner complete with observation decks and as many diversions as the passengers can afford. Bulk Cargo transportation would just need a big ship with powerful engines to move the cargo from place to place.

Regardless of the type of ship or the cargo it carries, the point of this mission is to move the cargo from point A to point B, while avoiding natural disasters as well as pirates and other obstacles.

Pirates

Piracy is a fact of life, but is difficult to explain outside of romantic ideals. In simplest of terms Pirates are thieves; they stop ships raid their cargo holds taking anything of value, sometimes including passengers, and then leave. Some times they leave their victim ships in tact, while other pirates may prefer to destroy the ship leaving no witnesses, some pirates stop their targets by destroying them outright assuming that anything valuable will survive to be salvaged after the fact.

Some pirates operate on behalf of a government; giving treaties to hunt and rob ships of rival nations. Other pirates are more charitable and operate in order to support the poor colony worlds they came from; while other pirates are just mean and rape, murder and pillage simply because they enjoy it.

The social and command structure on a pirate vessel is very different from a traditional military or corporate starship. While the average starship is pretty totalitarian with everyone following the Captain without question, pirate ships tend to operate democratically. The crew agrees to a set list of rules and guides when they sign on to the ship, and most decisions such as where to go or what ships to attack are decided by vote; but once combat begins the Captain is in full command. Ship postings are also voluntary on pirate ships, decided when each crewman signs on; if a crewman is a cook it is because they wanted to be a cook, not because that was the job they were assigned. Crew quarters are assigned in much the same way; there is no guarantee that the Captain will have the best cabin on the ship. It is also possible that the crew may elect someone different as the Captain if they don't like the way the current captain is handling things.